THE BRECON BEACO

D0231696

INCLUDING . . . **THE BLACK MOUNTAINS**

This guide book contains exact but simple directions for the motorist who wishes to combine visits to such well known places as Abergavenny, Brecon and Hay, with an exploration of the wide mountains and quiet valleys that lie hidden beyond the better known tourist routes.

The 'Main Circle Route' (Maps 1–14) shown on the Key Map opposite covers 163 miles and can be approached with ease from the Midlands and South Wales. This 'Main Circle Route' is of course much too long for a leisurely day's journey and we suggest that you use short lengths of main roads shown on the Key Map to make up your own shorter routes. The 'Link Route' on Map 15 follows a very narrow road up the lovely Honddu Valley and, preferably, should not be used during summer weekends when it could easily become congested.

HOW TO USE YOUR BOOK ON THE ROUTE

- Each double page makes up a complete picture of the country ahead of you. On the left you will find a one-inch-to-the-mile strip map, (apart from Map 15 which is approximately half an inch to the mile), with the route marked by a series of dashes. Direction is always from top to bottom, so that the map may be looked at in conjunction with the 'Directions', with which it is cross-referenced by a letter itemising most junction points. This enables the driver to have exact guidance every time an opportunity for changing direction occurs.

- With mileage intervals shown the driver has warning of when to expect 'moments of decision', and if a sign exists, we have used this to help you with the 'Signposted' column. However, some re-signing is always in progress and you would be advised to treat newly erected signs with some caution.

- We have included a description of the towns and villages through which you will pass, together with some photographs to illustrate the route.

- To gain full enjoyment from these journeys be prepared to leave your car as often as possible. The Brecon Beacons and the Black Mountains provide superb walking, both on open mountain country and along wooded valley bottoms, and to experience the true flavour of this lovely area, it is essential that you move away from the roads at every opportunity. **(However read notes on page 13 before wandering off into the hills.)** There is also a cave to be explored, waterfalls to be visited, and the ruins of Roman forts and medieval castles to be inspected; with the addition of a tree-shaded canal, several reservoirs, country inns and fascinating churches. So travel quietly, stop often, and take time to savour the delights of this remarkably diverse area in the true 'White Horse' way.

COMPILED BY PETER AND HELEN TITCHMARSH
PHOTOGRAPHY BY PETER TITCHMARSH

Map 1

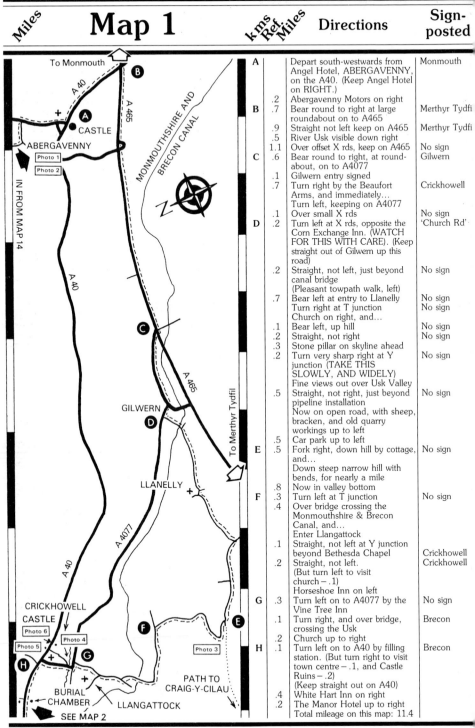

Miles	kms Ref. Miles	Directions	Sign-posted
A		Depart south-westwards from Angel Hotel, ABERGAVENNY, on the A40. (Keep Angel Hotel on RIGHT.)	Monmouth
	.2	Abergavenny Motors on right	
B	.7	Bear round to right at large roundabout on to A465	Merthyr Tydfi
	.9	Straight not left keep on A465	Merthyr Tydfi
	.5	River Usk visible down right	
	1.1	Over offset X rds, keep on A465	No sign
C	.6	Bear round to right, at round-about, on to A4077	Gilwern
	.1	Gilwern entry signed	
	.7	Turn right by the Beaufort Arms, and immediately...	Crickhowell
		Turn left, keeping on A4077	
	.1	Over small X rds	No sign
D	.2	Turn left at X rds, opposite the Corn Exchange Inn. (WATCH FOR THIS WITH CARE). (Keep straight out of Gilwern up this road)	'Church Rd'
	.2	Straight, not left, just beyond canal bridge (Pleasant towpath walk, left)	No sign
	.7	Bear left at entry to Llanelly	No sign
		Turn right at T junction	No sign
		Church on right, and...	
	.1	Bear left, up hill	No sign
	.2	Straight, not right	No sign
	.3	Stone pillar on skyline ahead	
	.2	Turn very sharp right at Y junction (TAKE THIS SLOWLY, AND WIDELY)	No sign
		Fine views out over Usk Valley	
	.5	Straight, not right, just beyond pipeline installation	No sign
		Now on open road, with sheep, bracken, and old quarry workings up to left	
	.5	Car park up to left	
E	.5	Fork right, down hill by cottage, and...	No sign
		Down steep narrow hill with bends, for nearly a mile	
	.8	Now in valley bottom	
F	.3	Turn left at T junction	No sign
	.4	Over bridge crossing the Monmouthshire & Brecon Canal, and...	
		Enter Llangattock	
	.1	Straight, not left at Y junction beyond Bethesda Chapel	Crickhowell
	.2	Straight, not left. (But turn left to visit church – .1)	Crickhowell
		Horseshoe Inn on left	
G	.3	Turn left on to A4077 by the Vine Tree Inn	No sign
	.1	Turn right, and over bridge, crossing the Usk	Brecon
	.2	Church up to right	
H	.1	Turn left on to A40 by filling station. (But turn right to visit town centre – .1, and Castle Ruins – .2) (Keep straight out on A40)	Brecon
	.4	White Hart Inn on right	
	.2	The Manor Hotel up to right	
		Total mileage on this map: 11.4	

The Clyddach Valley to Crickhowell

Abergavenny

Busy market town and tourist centre overlooked by the mountains between which the lovely River Usk flows... the Blorenge to the south, the Sugar Loaf to the north-west and the Skirrid to the north-east. The Romans, who soon realised the strategic importance of this site established a fort here known as Gobannium and the Normans had built a castle by about 1090. The castle ruins are pleasantly sited on the southern edge of the town looking out over the Usk valley towards the Blorenge, and incorporate an interesting small museum and an early 19th century 'keep'. St. Mary's church, in Monk Street, was largely rebuilt in the 19th century, but it contains a bewilderingly large assortment of monuments including a fine 13th century wooden effigy of a knight and an effigy of Jesse, also in wood, which must have once been the base of a 'Jesse Tree' reredos. Take time off to explore the busy and colourful streets, especially Market Street with its little arcaded shops. There is a National Park Information Centre at Swan Meadow, Monmouth Road.

Gilwern

The Monmouthshire and Brecon Canal crosses the little River Clydach over a tall wooded embankment above the village, and the towpath (to the left of our road) is well worth exploring.

Llanelly

Quiet hamlet on a high hillside overlooking the Usk valley, with an over restored church standing in a large rather neglected churchyard.

Mynydd Llangattock

Our moorland road follows the course of an old tramway linking the great limestone quarries on the escarpment to our left, with the ironworks of the Clydach valley and Nantyglo*. The line of the tramway may be explored on foot beyond Point E, below the rocky escarpment towards Craig-y-Cilau and Agen Allwedd (the keyhole), which however must only be explored by experts.
*Read Alexander Cordell's fine novel *Rape of the Fair Country* and Chris Barber's book, *Cordell Country*.

Llangattock

Pleasant village with early 19th century houses lining the quiet street to the church. This stout towered building has been much restored, but it does contain the old village stocks and whipping post, and an attractive series of 18th and 19th century monuments.

Crickhowell

Colourful little market town with a lovely 13 arch medieval bridge over the Usk. The much restored church has a fine 17th century monument and two medieval effigies, and to the east of the town are the scanty remains of a medieval castle. The Manor Hotel (see Route Directions) was the birthplace in 1790 of Sir George Everest, the Surveyor General of India, after whom the world's highest mountain was named.

1. The King's Arms, Abergavenny

2. Classical elegance, Abergavenny

3. Our road above Llangattock (beyond Point E.)

4. Crickhowell Bridge

5. The Bear Hotel, Crickhowell

6. Crickhowell Castle

Ref	Miles	Directions	Sign-posted
	.2	Straight, not left, keeping on A40	No sign
	.1	Straight, not right, keeping on A40	No sign
A	.7	Fork right, on to A479 by Cider Mill Inn	Builth Wells
	.1	Straight, not right, keeping on A479	No sign
	1.0	Tretower entry signed, and... Straight, not right	No sign
B	.1	Turn left, off A479, and... (BUT GO STRAIGHT AHEAD ON A479 FOR 9 MILES IF YOU WISH TO LINK ON TO MAP 10 AT TALGARTH) Fork left by church	'Tretower Court' / No sign
	.1	Tretower Court and Castle on right	
C	.4	Turn left with care on to A40	No sign
	.2	Turn right, with care, off A40, and into pleasant woodlands (private)	Gliffaes
	1.0	Entrance to Gliffaes Hotel on left	
	1.5	Turn left at T junction	No sign
D	.3	Turn left at X rds on to B4560	No sign
	.2	Llangynidr entry signed	
	.2	Over Llangynidr Bridge crossing River Usk	
	.1	Straight, not right	'Forge Rd'
	.1	Over canal bridge, and... Straight, not right	'Forge Rd'
E	.2	Turn sharp right, on to B4558	Talybont
	.3	Over small diagonal X rds keeping on B4558	No sign
	.2	Bear left by Coach & Horses	Talybont
F	.1	Straight, not left, keeping on B4558	No sign
	1.1	Llanddetty Church on right	
	.9	Canal on left... enters Ashford Tunnel	
	.2	Canal re-emerges from tunnel. Parking space on left	
	.4	Talybont entry signed	
	.2	Over small X rds beyond Traveller's Rest. (But turn sharp left if you wish to explore up mountain road beneath Tor-y-Foel – 2.5)	
G	.1	Straight, not right, and under old railway bridge	Pencelli
	.2	Left at T junction, and... Over lift bridge crossing canal	Torpantau
H	.4	Bear left at Y junction, on to wider road	No sign
	.1	Straight, not right	No sign
	.5	Aber entry signed	
	.3	Information Centre, etc on left	
	.4	Talybont Reservoir dam to left. (Turn left if you wish to cross dam, and take 1st turn right beyond dam, for quiet track overlooking reservoir. Motorable for short distance only)	
	.7	Car Park on left	
	.1	Talybont Forest sign on right, and enter woodlands	
		Total mileage on this map: 12.7	

Beside the Monmouthshire and Brecon Canal

Tretower

Do not miss a visit to Tretower Court, an unusually well preserved medieval house built around a central courtyard, with 17th century additions. Beyond the Court are the remains of a castle... a circular tower rising from the ruins of a 12th century keep. The little 19th century church close by is the work of one of our favourites, J. L. Pearson, the architect of Truro Cathedral.

1. Tretower Castle

Llangynidr Bridge

A lovely late medieval, six arch stone bridge over the sparkling River Usk, along the south banks of which there are splendid walks, both to left and right.

The Monmouthshire and Brecon Canal

This was authorised by an Act of Parliament in 1793 and construction took place between 1797 and 1812, when the final link between Brecon and the Monmouth Canal was completed. Various tramroads were built to link with the canal in the years that followed, mainly for the purpose of feeding the ironworks in the valleys to the south, but for details read the National Park leaflet 'The Pattern of Past Industry'. The 32 mile stretch between Pontypool and Brecon is now in active use for leisure purposes and provides safe and relaxed cruising on the lovely southern slopes of the Usk valley.

2. Tretower Court

Llanddetty Church

Small building between the road and the steep wooded banks of the Usk. A lovely old door opens into a rather musty interior, with pleasant barrel-vaulted ceiling and primitive Royal Arms of one of the Georges painted on the north wall.

Mountain Diversion beneath Tor-y-Foel

Turn sharp left just beyond the Traveller's Rest in Talybont if you wish to drive up on to the mountainside beneath Tor-y-Foel for splendid views out over Talybont Reservoir. It is possible to walk from here over the hills to Pontsticill. Parking space limited, but well worth trying.

3. Our road towards Llangynidr

Talybont

This has at least three inns, and a chapel, but for all this, it is not our favourite Brecon Beacons village. Perhaps the best place to stop awhile is at the white painted canal lift bridge, where you may be able to watch your water-borne brethren grapple with the bridge (this may in any case be an involuntary stop for you, but make the most of it).

Talybont Reservoir

We first come upon the little Information Centre, with its toilets, camp and picnic site, map of the whole area showing car parks, paths, etc. Half a mile beyond is the grass covered dam, from the top of which there are fine views up the reservoir to the hills beyond.

4. Llangynidr Bridge

Map 3

Map labels:
- Photo 1 — BLAEN-Y-GLYN FALLS
- CAR PARK
- Photo 2 — TORPANTAU (A)
- (B)
- OWL'S GROVE CAR PARK & PICNIC SITE
- PENTWYN RESERVOIR (C)
- (D)
- PONTSTICILL RESERVOIR
- CAR PARK
- RAILWAY STATION — Photo 3 (E)
- WATER TREATMENT WORKS
- PONTSTICILL
- (F)
- VAYNOR CHURCH
- HY BRASAIL
- MOUND — Photo 4
- PONTSARN VIADUCT
- MORLAIS CASTLE
- (G)
- DAREN FÂCH
- VAYNOR QUARRY
- PONTSARN VIADUCT
- SEE MAP 4
- A 470
- A 465
- (H)
- CEFN-COED-Y-CYMMER
- To the Taf Fechan Valley
- To Abergavenny
- To Swansea
- To Merthyr Tydfil

	kms Ref Miles	Directions	Sign-posted
	1.1	Head of reservoir on left	
	.8	Over bridge with farm on right	
	1.2	Over Caerfanell stream	
A	.1	Good car park on left. (Forest Trail up to right leading to Blaen-y-glyn waterfall – .2)	
	.1	Climb up steeply from here	
	.2	Glimpse of waterfall well over to right	
	.2	Over cattle-grid and on to open country	
	.2	Path to waterfall on right	
	.4	Garn Fawr visible to right	
B	.3	Straight, not left at summit of road. Now start descending	No sign
	.4	Cross old railway line near site of Torpantau Station and into forest country	
	.1	Parking area on right	
	.2	Taf Fechan car park and picnic site on left	
C	.4	Turn left at T junction (But turn right if you wish to explore up Taf Fechan valley. Total road length – 1.8)	Pontsticill
	.1	Pentwyn Reservoir visible ahead	
	.8	Small Victorian church to left	
D	.1	Turn right at T junction (But turn left for fine view up reservoir after – .2)	Pontsticill
	.8	Car park on left	
	.7	Water Works on left	
	.2	Bear sharp left at Y junction	Dowlais
	.2	Over Pontsticill Reservoir dam. Valve tower to left	
E	.2	Turn right beyond dam (But turn left if you wish to visit Brecon Mountain Railway H.Q. if now open to visitors)	No sign
	.4	Turn sharp right at Y junction	No sign
	.3	Bear left on to wider road by Red Cow Inn, Pontsticill	No sign
	.2	Straight, not left, beyond Butchers Arms	No sign
F	.7	Bear half right at X rds, keeping on wider road (But go slightly left if you wish to visit Vaynor church – .2)	No sign
	.3	Hy Brasail on right, and… Small mound down track left	
	.2	Pontsarn Viaduct visible down to left	
	.1	Pontsarn Inn on left	
G	.1	Bear round to right at T junction by the Aber Glais Inn (But turn left if you wish to park after .2 and walk up valley beneath viaduct)	Cefn Coed
	.6	Quarry entrance to right	
	.1	Entering 'built-up' area	
H	.9	Turn right with care on to A470 in Cefn-Coed	Brecon
	.7	Fine views ahead as we leave 'built-up' area	
	.5	Crags of Daren Fâch on right Total mileage on this map: 13.7	

Great reservoirs and a mountain railway

The Brecon and Merthyr Railway

This was opened in 1865, and although closed in 1963, it is still traceable over most of its course.

Blaen-y-Glyn Waterfalls

These are delightfully situated (as their Welsh name tells us) in a 'glen at the head of the valley'. There is an 'honesty box' at the nearby car park, with copies of an inexpensive leaflet describing the 'Talybont Forest Trail', a series of inter-connected walks past several waterfalls. (Stout shoes please).

1. The lowest waterfall, Blaen-y-Glyn

Torpantau

This marks our summit, and is fine walking country. The old B. & M. Railway went through a tunnel beneath here, and re-emerged near Torpantau Station, the site of which is still visible on our right.

Taf Fechan Forest Car Park...

Lywyn-y-Dylluan (Owl's Grove)

There is a forest walk from this point, details of which are described on a displayed map.

Diversion up the Taf Fechan Valley

There are two Forestry Commission car parks on this road up towards the Neuadd Reservoirs, but the public road goes less than two miles and stops just short of the first reservoir.

2. Our road near the Torpantau 'summit'

Pentwyn and Pontsticill Reservoirs

There are fine views of these from the bridge between them, which is to our left at Point D.

Pontsticill

The impressive new water treatment works provide an interesting architectural contrast with the Rhineland-Gothic valve tower in the reservoir beyond and the domed buildings below the dam. The old Brecon & Merthyr railway station beyond the dam is now the H.Q. of the developing Brecon Mountain Railway, which is operative between Pant and Pontsticill Reservoir. The village of Pontsticill itself has several pleasant terraces of stone cottages.

Vaynor

Here is Hy Brasail, a fascinating house in the Italian style, dated 1912, a churchyard with views down the valley through cypress trees and a dark little Victorian church. This was built by ironmaster, Robert Crawshay, whose massive tomb slab in the churchyard is inscribed 'God Forgive Me'. Judging from his reputation locally, this was perhaps a plea worth making.

3. Brecon Mountain Railway — Loco in steam.
(Photo, courtesy of Brecon Mountain Railway.)

Pontsarn Viaduct

A fine example of Victorian civil engineering (1866) which may be viewed from beneath, by diverting at Point G.

Morlais Castle

To the east of Pontsarn are the splendidly sited, but fragmentary ruins of this medieval castle, but they are difficult to spot from our road.

4. Sunshine at Vaynor

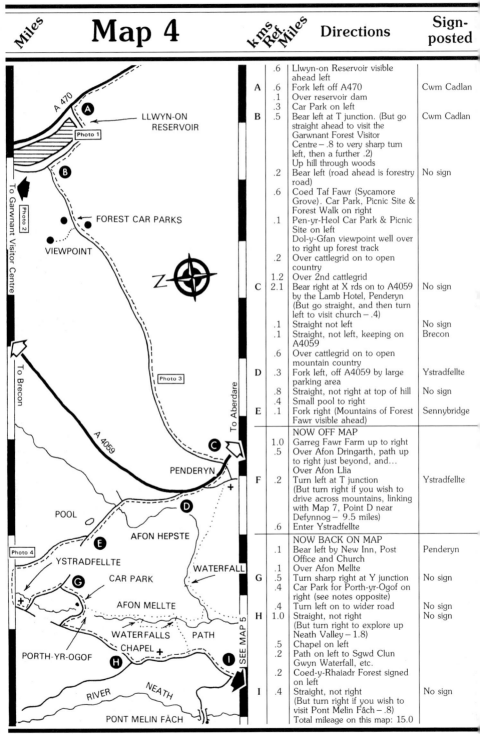

	kms	Ref	Miles	Directions	Sign-posted
			.6	Llwyn-on Reservoir visible ahead left	
		A	.6	Fork left off A470	Cwm Cadlan
			.1	Over reservoir dam	
			.3	Car Park on left	
		B	.5	Bear left at T junction. (But go straight ahead to visit the Garwnant Forest Visitor Centre – .8 to very sharp turn left, then a further .2) Up hill through woods	Cwm Cadlan
			.2	Bear left (road ahead is forestry road)	No sign
			.6	Coed Taf Fawr (Sycamore Grove). Car Park, Picnic Site & Forest Walk on right	
			.1	Pen-yr-Heol Car Park & Picnic Site on left Dol-y-Gfan viewpoint well over to right up forest track	
			.2	Over cattlegrid on to open country	
			1.2	Over 2nd cattlegrid	
		C	2.1	Bear right at X rds on to A4059 by the Lamb Hotel, Penderyn (But go straight, and then turn left to visit church – .4)	No sign
			.1	Straight not left	No sign
			.1	Straight, not left, keeping on A4059	Brecon
			.6	Over cattlegrid on to open mountain country	
		D	.3	Fork left, off A4059 by large parking area	Ystradfellte
			.8	Straight, not right at top of hill	No sign
			.4	Small pool to right	
		E	.1	Fork right (Mountains of Forest Fawr visible ahead)	Sennybridge
				NOW OFF MAP	
			1.0	Garreg Fawr Farm up to right	
			.5	Over Afon Dringarth, path up to right just beyond, and... Over Afon Llia	
		F	.2	Turn left at T junction (But turn right if you wish to drive across mountains, linking with Map 7, Point D near Defynnog – 9.5 miles)	Ystradfellte
			.6	Enter Ystradfellte	
				NOW BACK ON MAP	
			.1	Bear left by New Inn, Post Office and Church	Penderyn
			.1	Over Afon Mellte	
		G	.5	Turn sharp right at Y junction	No sign
			.4	Car Park for Porth-yr-Ogof on right (see notes opposite)	
			.4	Turn left on to wider road	No sign
		H	1.0	Straight, not right (But turn right to explore up Neath Valley – 1.8)	No sign
			.5	Chapel on left	
			.2	Path on left to Sgwd Clun Gwyn Waterfall, etc.	
			.2	Coed-y-Rhaiadr Forest signed on left	
		I	.4	Straight, not right (But turn right if you wish to visit Pont Melin Fâch – .8) Total mileage on this map: 15.0	No sign

8

Mountains, forests and a disappearing river

Llwyn-on (Ash Grove) Reservoir

The largest and most southerly of a string of three reservoirs in the Taf Fawr valley, having dense Forestry Commission woodlands on almost every side. Boat permits for day fishermen may be purchased at the water treatment works below the dam.

Garwnant Forest Centre

This most interesting Forestry Commission facility provides a wealth of information on the forestry scene in a most attractive way. There are maps and leaflets available, and a circular forest walk.

Penderyn

A sad little village with fine views from its churchyard, but little else of interest.

Castell Coch (The Red Castle)

This was a medieval castle... possibly a hunting lodge for the Fforest Fawr, the hunting grounds of the Lords of Brecon. All that now remains are a collection of red sandstone boulders (hence the name) on a wooded mound to our right.

Mountain Road Link from Point F to Map 7, Point D.

Drive at least 3.5 miles northwards to pass the great flat standing stone, Maen Llia, on your right... and just beyond, to the head of the dramatic descent down the steep northern scarp.

Ystradfellte

Attractive little village in the lovely Mellte valley, with an inn, a post office stores and a moderately interesting church. The interior of this has been over restored, but the old stone floors remain, and there are several pleasant memorial tablets in the chancel.

Porth-yr-Ogof and the Mellte and Hepste Valley Waterfalls

Here the River Mellte disappears into a 1,400 foot long cavern, and it is possible to view its entry and then walk south along the old river bed above the line of the cave, to the point where the river re-emerges. Walk further southwards and cross a bridge if you wish to visit the waterfalls of Sgwd Clun-Gwyn, Sgwd Clun-Gwyn Isaf and Sgwd-y-Pannwr, and possibly re-join our road route beyond Point H. If you wish to visit Sgwd-yr-Eira waterfall on the tributary Hepste, follow the path down the east side of the valley before crossing the bridge, and head up the beautifully wooded Hepste valley. All these directions inevitably appear confusing and if at all possible you should use the 1:25,000 O.S. Leisure Map, Brecon Beacons (Central Area). This is one of a set of three covering almost the whole area of the National Park, which are invaluable companions.

The Neath (or Nedd) Valley

This two mile diversion takes us past a pleasant farmhouse, with pond (Berth-Lwyd), to a minute parking space, a short distance from a bridge over the River Neath. Close by there is a cave, but this should NOT be explored.

Pont Melin-Fâch, The Neath and Pyrddin Waterfalls (See page 13)

1. Fishing boats on Lwyn-On Reservoir

2. Display at Garwnant Forest Visitor Centre

3. Mountain ponies near Penderyn

4. Mountain Link Road north of Ystradfellte

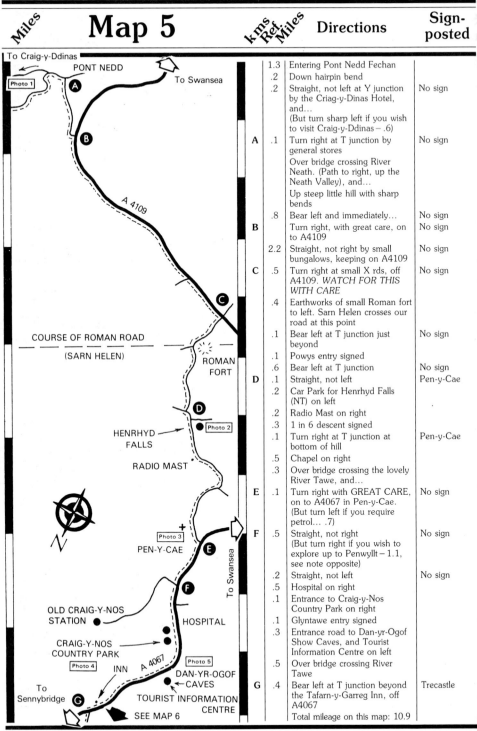

Ref	Miles	Directions	Sign-posted
	1.3	Entering Pont Nedd Fechan	
	.2	Down hairpin bend	
	.2	Straight, not left at Y junction by the Criag-y-Dinas Hotel, and… (But turn sharp left if you wish to visit Craig-y-Ddinas – .6)	No sign
A	.1	Turn right at T junction by general stores	No sign
		Over bridge crossing River Neath. (Path to right, up the Neath Valley), and…	
		Up steep little hill with sharp bends	
	.8	Bear left and immediately…	No sign
B		Turn right, with great care, on to A4109	No sign
	2.2	Straight, not right by small bungalows, keeping on A4109	No sign
C	.5	Turn right at small X rds, off A4109. *WATCH FOR THIS WITH CARE*	No sign
	.4	Earthworks of small Roman fort to left. Sarn Helen crosses our road at this point	
	.1	Bear left at T junction just beyond	No sign
	.1	Powys entry signed	
	.6	Bear left at T junction	No sign
D	.1	Straight, not left	Pen-y-Cae
	.2	Car Park for Henrhyd Falls (NT) on left	
	.2	Radio Mast on right	
	.3	1 in 6 descent signed	
	.1	Turn right at T junction at bottom of hill	Pen-y-Cae
	.5	Chapel on right	
	.3	Over bridge crossing the lovely River Tawe, and…	
E	.1	Turn right with GREAT CARE, on to A4067 in Pen-y-Cae. (But turn left if you require petrol… .7)	No sign
F	.5	Straight, not right (But turn right if you wish to explore up to Penwyllt – 1.1, see note opposite)	No sign
	.2	Straight, not left	No sign
	.5	Hospital on right	
	.1	Entrance to Craig-y-Nos Country Park on right	
	.1	Glyntawe entry signed	
	.3	Entrance road to Dan-yr-Ogof Show Caves, and Tourist Information Centre on left	
	.5	Over bridge crossing River Tawe	
G	.4	Bear left at T junction beyond the Tafarn-y-Garreg Inn, off A4067	Trecastle
		Total mileage on this map: 10.9	

To Craig-y-Ddinas
PONT NEDD
Photo 1
To Swansea
A 4109
COURSE OF ROMAN ROAD
(SARN HELEN)
ROMAN FORT
HENRHYD FALLS
Photo 2
RADIO MAST
Photo 3
PEN-Y-CAE
To Swansea
OLD CRAIG-Y-NOS STATION
HOSPITAL
CRAIG-Y-NOS COUNTRY PARK
Photo 4
INN
A 4067
Photo 5
DAN-YR-OGOF CAVES
To Sennybridge
TOURIST INFORMATION CENTRE
SEE MAP 6

Scenery and song... and a massive cave too

Pont Nedd Fechan and Craig-y-Ddinas

Quiet village just to the north of the busy A465, Heads of the Valley road. It is possible to walk from here up the west bank of the river Neath to its confluence with the Pyrddin, near which are several fine waterfalls (see Pont Melin-Fâch, pages 9, 13). Follow our route directions for Craig-y-Ddinas, a dramatic limestone crag, in a pleasantly wooded area beside the Mellte river.

Coelbren Roman Fort and Sarn Helen

Here are the unimpressive earthworks of a small Roman fort, linked by a Roman road, the Sarn Helen, to the large fort of Brecon Gaer (see page 17). They were probably both built during the governorship of Frontinus in about AD 74, as part of his plan to subjugate the Celtic tribes of South Wales, the Silures. Much of Sarn Helen's course can still be traced and its earth bank or agger is particularly clear to the east of Coelbren fort (to the right of our road).

Henrhyd Waterfall (N.T.)

There is a steep path down through woods to reach this dramatic waterfall, where the river Llech falls ninety feet over a sheer cliff in which is exposed a thin seam of coal. The effort is worthwhile.

Penwyllt—a diversion for 'enthusiasts' only

The diversion road up to the large quarries was originally made on the instructions of Madame Patti (see Craig-y-Nos below), so that she could easily reach the little railway halt, where she had a specially furnished waiting room. This is not open to the public and the quarry road traffic is heavy enough to discourage all but the most enthusiastic.

Craig-y-Nos and Craig-y-Nos Country Park

This great Victorian 'castle' was the home of Madame Adelina Patti, the internationally famous opera 'star' from 1878 until her death in 1919. The grounds through which the river Tawe flows have been incorporated into a most attractive Country Park, with two lakes, many fine trees and an interesting little Information Room (buy the leaflet Scenery and Song at Craig-y-Nos'—all about Madame Patti's life here).

Dan-yr-Ogof Caves, etc.

This consists of Dan-yr-Ogof 'showcave', the 'largest showcave in Britain', and the Cathedral Cave, which has the 'largest chamber of any British showcave'. A conducted tour of both caves takes about one and half hours. There is an interpretive museum with an emphasis on caves, geology and prehistory; a shop, restaurant, motel and caravan and camping site; and also, on the hillside just above, a fascinating assortment of life-size prehistoric beasts.

1. Craig-y-Ddinas   2. Henrhyd Waterfall

3. The River Tawe near Pen-y-Cae

4. At Craig-y-Nos Country Park

5. Prehistoric beasts at Dan-yr-Ogof

11

		kms Ref. Miles	Directions	Sign-posted
		1.4	Over cattlegrid. Road on left now unfenced	
			Now on an attractive mountain road following up beside the infant River Tawe	
Photo 1		.7	Footpath to Fan Foel to left (not easily identifiable)	
STONE CIRCLE				
STANDING STONE		.2	Small waterfall to left	
Photo 2				
STANDING STONE		.1	Cerrig Duon stone circle and Maen Mawr standing stone visible back left (not easily identifiable)	
			Fine views to left of the Fan Foel crags	
Photo 3		.5	Standing stone visible up to right	
GLAS FYNYDD		.5	Distant views over to the right as we cross the south/north watershed	
FOREST		.8	Over cattlegrid into Glas Fynydd Forest	
Ⓐ	A	.6	Straight, not right at T junction	No sign
		.1	Bear right at next T junction	No sign
Ⓑ		.7	Now leaving forest	
	B	.6	Straight, not left at T junction	No sign
Ⓒ	C	.6	Bear right at T junction (But turn left if you wish to visit the Usk Reservoir. After .5 straight not left beyond Pont-ar-Hydfer church. After .3 straight, not right. After .6 bear right at T junction. After 1.3 turn right at T junction. After 1.0 arrive at car park by dam. TOTAL MILEAGE 3.7. Then turnabout and return to Point C)	Trecastle
PONT-AR-HYDFER				
SEE MAP 7				
Photo 4		.1	Water treatment works on right	
CAR PARK			Total mileage on this map (excluding diversion to the Usk Reservoir): 6.9	
USK RESERVOIR				

N

In the heart of the Beacons

The Upper Tawe Valley

Our quiet road northwards from the Taffarn-y-Garreg Inn follows the infant River Tawe almost to its source below Llyn-y-Fan-Fawr and the great crags of Fan Foel. There are several small waterfalls and at one point, not far beyond the stream, there is a small Bronze Age stone circle... Cerrig Duon, with a large standing stone, Maen Mawr, just to its north-west, complete with a rough avenue of stones close by. There is another standing stone, up to our right about half a mile beyond. But just before reaching any of these remains there is an ill defined path (not signed) to the left leading up to Llyn-y-Fan-Fawr and Fan Foel... but read note at bottom of this page before attempting any hill walking.

Glas Fynydd Forest

We now drop down towards the Usk Valley and forsake the open mountain country for the Forestry Commission's Glas Fynydd Forest. This is not one of our favourite forests, but it looks pleasant enough on a fine sunny day.

The Usk Reservoir

This is nearly four miles off our main route, but the road to it is excellent, and although the dam itself is a very dull looking structure, the tree lined shores of the reservoir are most attractive. (Access appears to be fairly restricted.)

Pont Melin-Fâch and The Neath and Pyrddin Waterfalls (See page 8)

Here is a delightful tree shaded parking area and picnic site in the lovely Neath Valley. Walk down the far (western) bank of the Neath, past several fine waterfalls, to the point where the Neath is joined by the River Pyrddin. If you walk up the Pyrddin for a short distance you will reach the splendid Sgwd Gwladys or Lady's Fall, and beyond it, the eighty foot Sgwd Einion Gam waterfall. (Use 1:25,000 Outdoor Leisure Map... Brecon Beacons... Central Area.)

PLEASE READ THESE NOTES BEFORE SETTING OUT ON ANY EXPEDITIONS

Mountain Walking

Use good maps, preferably the Ordnance Survey 1:25,000 Outdoor Leisure Maps, which cover the National Park area in three sheets. Use stout footwear and even in summer, take warm water-proof clothing, as exposure can be fatal. Always leave word where you are going. Seek general advice and maps from the Mountain Centre (see page 15).

Caving

Do not attempt this except with an experienced club. Go instead to Dan-yr-Ogof Caves (see page 11).

Motoring, Picnicking, etc.

Drive slowly. Leave gates as you find them, but if in doubt close them. Do not leave litter. Do not drive or park on commons, away from the road... it is illegal. Do keep dogs under close control. Sorry to mention these all too obvious points, but perhaps this is the first 'By Car' book that you have used.

1. Fan Foel in winter

2. Summer in the Upper Tawe Valley

3. Our road through Glas Fynydd Forest

4. Snowy afternoon at Usk Reservoir

Map 7

Map illustration showing route from To Llandovery, TRECASTLE, PANTYSGALLOG BRIDGE (Photo 2), PARKING SPACE, To Swansea, A 4067 (Photo 1), SENNY BRIDGE, DEFYNNOG, LINK ROAD TO MAP 4, POINT F, A 4215, To Brecon, To Merthyr Tydfil, CASTLE MOUND, POOL (Photo 3), MYNYDD ILLTUD COMMON, LLANILLTUD CHURCH, MOUNTAIN CENTRE (Photo 4, Photo 5), SEE MAP 8. Points A, B, C, D, E, F marked along route with A 40 road.

	Miles	Directions	Sign-posted
A	1.1	Turn sharp right at T junction (But go straight ahead if you wish to visit Trecastle – .2)	Cray
	.3	Bear left at Y junction	Cray
	1.0	Bear left at Y junction	No sign
	.1	Down very steep hill	
	.1	Turn left at T junction	Sennybridge
B	1.1	Bear right at T junction (But turn left, park, and walk down road to left if you wish to visit Pantysgallog Bridge – .4)	Sennybridge
	.7	Straight, not left at T junction	No sign
	.4	Cross line of old railway	
C	.3	Turn right at small X rds on to A4067 in Defynnog	No sign
	.1	Lion Inn on right	
		Church down to right	
	.1	Turn left at T junction, on to A4215	Merthyr Tydfil
D	.9	Straight, not right (Road to right makes fine mountain link route to Ystradfellte, at Map 4, Point F – 9.5)	Mountain Centre
	.3	Lay-by Car Park on left	
	.3	Fine views of Brecon Beacons ahead	
	.3	Straight, not left	Mountain Centre
E	.3	Turn left at X rds off A4215	'Light Vehicles Only'
	.6	Over small stream	
	.1	Straight, not left	
	.2	Over cattlegrid on to Mynydd Illtud Common. (No parking or picnicking – drive on to Mountain Centre and explore from there)	
		Castle mound visible over to left	
		Pool on right	
	.4	Over stream. Fine views of Brecon Beacons up to right	
	.2	Straight, not left at Y junction	No sign
F	.3	Straight, not right at T junction	No sign
		(BUT TURN RIGHT IF YOU WISH TO VISIT MOUNTAIN CENTRE, WHICH IS HIGHLY RECOMMENDED – .6)	
		(Then return to main route at Point F)	
		Total mileage on this map: 9.2	

Open country below the Beacons

Trecastle

Astride the A40, this pleasant village must have been a busy coaching halt in the days before the railways, for there are at least three inns still, and there is at least one other house which must have been a coaching inn. At the upper, eastern end of the village stands the prominent tree covered mound of the old castle.

Pantysgallog Bridge

Lovely old single arch bridge over the infant Usk. Park near our main route and walk down to the bridge to look upstream to the little waterfall. A notice declares... 'No fishing, boating, bathing or picnicking'... but it is still worth leaning over the bridge.

Defynnog

A scattered village with a row of Gothick cottages, an inn and a tall towered church looking westwards over a valley to the hills of Fforest Fach. The Victorianised, shiny tiled interior contains a font ornamented with a Runic inscription, the only known specimen in Wales; and a 5th or 6th century inscribed stone built into the base of the tower.

Mynydd Illtud Common

This is a delightful open area with a pool close to our road and a small stream some distance beyond. We suggest that you drive on to the Mountain Centre and explore from there using the leaflet about the centre, which incorporates a clear map and description of the features to be found on the common.

Llanilltud Church

This lies to the right of our diversion road to the Mountain Centre... a sadly neglected little early Victorian building, with broken windows and bird droppings much in evidence... all in rather disturbing contrast to the care lavished upon the Mountain Centre.

The Brecon Beacons Mountain Centre

This low white walled building was opened in 1966 and is an outstanding example of what can be done to enrich a visit to a National Park. Here will be found a most interesting Information Room complete with displays and a small shop selling books and maps, a well organised buffet restaurant, and a verandah and balcony terrace from whence there are splendid views over to the Beacons. There is usually ample parking space (for which there is a charge), and several interesting paths radiate from here. DO NOT MISS A VISIT... PREFERABLY EARLY IN YOUR EXPLORATION OF THE AREA.

Twyn-y-Gaer (See page 16)

Iron Age hill fort to the north of Mynydd Illtud Common, on a promontory overlooking the Usk valley. There are fine views from the 1,200 foot summit.

Aberbran (See page 16)

Pleasant hamlet with a charming 18th century bridge over the little Nant Bran, a short distance above its confluence with the Usk.

1. Defynnog Church   2. Pantysgallog Bridge

3. Winter feed-time on Mynydd Illtud Common

4. Information Room at the Mountain Centre

5. The Beacons from our route beyond the Mountain Centre

Map 8

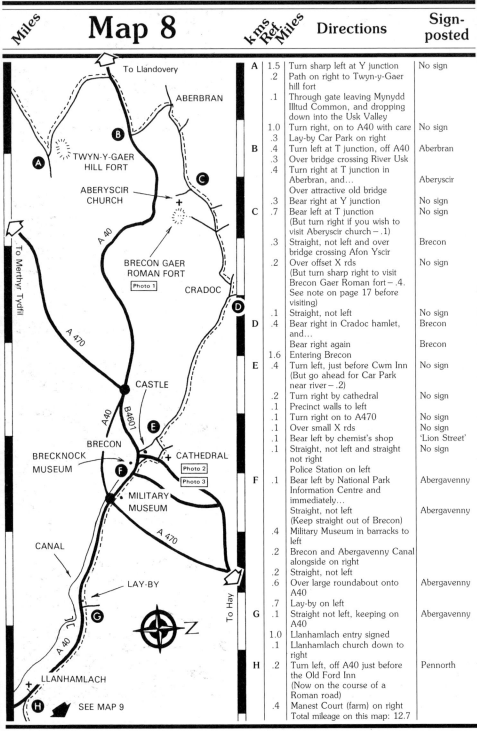

Miles				Map 8	kms Ref. Miles	Directions	Sign-posted

Ref	kms/Miles	Directions	Sign-posted
A	1.5	Turn sharp left at Y junction	No sign
	.2	Path on right to Twyn-y-Gaer hill fort	
	.1	Through gate leaving Mynydd Illtud Common, and dropping down into the Usk Valley	
	1.0	Turn right, on to A40 with care	No sign
	.3	Lay-by Car Park on right	
B	.4	Turn left at T junction, off A40	Aberbran
	.3	Over bridge crossing River Usk	
	.4	Turn right at T junction in Aberbran, and…	Aberyscir
		Over attractive old bridge	
C	.3	Bear right at Y junction	No sign
	.7	Bear left at T junction (But turn right if you wish to visit Aberyscir church – .1)	No sign
	.3	Straight, not left and over bridge crossing Afon Yscir	Brecon
	.2	Over offset X rds (But turn sharp right to visit Brecon Gaer Roman fort – .4. See note on page 17 before visiting)	No sign
	.1	Straight, not left	No sign
D	.4	Bear right in Cradoc hamlet, and…	Brecon
		Bear right again	Brecon
	1.6	Entering Brecon	
E	.4	Turn left, just before Cwm Inn (But go ahead for Car Park near river – .2)	No sign
	.2	Turn right by cathedral	No sign
	.1	Precinct walls to left	
	.1	Turn right on to A470	No sign
	.1	Over small X rds	No sign
	.1	Bear left by chemist's shop	'Lion Street'
	.1	Straight, not left and straight not right	No sign
		Police Station on left	
F	.1	Bear left by National Park Information Centre and immediately…	Abergavenny
		Straight, not left (Keep straight out of Brecon)	Abergavenny
	.4	Military Museum in barracks to left	
	.2	Brecon and Abergavenny Canal alongside on right	
	.2	Straight, not left	
	.6	Over large roundabout onto A40	Abergavenny
	.7	Lay-by on left	
G	.1	Straight not left, keeping on A40	Abergavenny
	1.0	Llanhamlach entry signed	
	.1	Llanhamlach church down to right	
H	.2	Turn left, off A40 just before the Old Ford Inn (Now on the course of a Roman road)	Pennorth
	.4	Manest Court (farm) on right	
		Total mileage on this map: 12.7	

To Llandovery

ABERBRAN

TWYN-Y-GAER HILL FORT

ABERYSCIR CHURCH

A 40

BRECON GAER ROMAN FORT

Photo 1

CRADOC

To Merthyr Tydfil

A 470

CASTLE

B4601

A40

BRECON

BRECKNOCK MUSEUM

CATHEDRAL

Photo 2

Photo 3

MILITARY MUSEUM

A 470

CANAL

LAY-BY

To Hay

N

LLANHAMLACH

SEE MAP 9

A Roman fort and an old county town

Twyn-y-Gaer and Aberbran (See page 15)

1. At Brecon Gaer

Aberyscir and Brecon Gaer

Minute hamlet with a quiet little Victorian church standing above the point where the Yscir flows into the Usk. Beyond the Yscir lie the remains of the great Roman fort of Brecon Gaer or Y Gaer. (Turn sharp right .2 beyond bridge over Afon Yscir and motor up farm drive [not signed]. Stop at farmhouse to purchase interesting booklet, park where directed and walk beyond farmyard.) This was probably built about AD 74, as the hub of a network of smaller forts (see Coelbren, page 11). Parts of the walls and three of the gateways may be inspected, although access is limited during May, June and July in view of possible damage to the hay crop.

Brecon

The pleasant county town of the old county of Brecon stands at the confluence of the Usk and the Honddu rivers, hence its Welsh name Aberhonddu, the mouth of the Honddu. This confluence is just below the ruins of a medieval castle, now incorporated into the Castle of Brecon Hotel, and which overlooks the riverside car park easily reached from our route (Point E). Walk from the bridge by the car park, along the 'Promenade', a pleasant tree shaded walk along the north bank of the Usk.

Brecon Cathedral only achieved its present status in 1923, but it is a dignified old cruciform building with a stout central tower and an interior on a substantial scale. This contains several items of interest including a wooden Elizabethan effigy and a fine alabaster tomb of the same period. A path through the churchyard leads to Priory Groves, which slopes down towards the Honddu, and there is a Nature Trail about a mile and a half long which is well worth following.

The old Shire Hall now houses the most interesting Brecknock Museum and there is a National Park Information Centre at Watton Mount opposite. Between the Museum and the river there is the Captain's Walk', named after Napoleonic prisoners who took their exercise here, and just beyond is the head of the lovely Monmouthshire and Brecon Canal (see page 5). Do not miss a visit to the South Wales Borderers' Museum (in the Watton, the street that takes us out of the town) with its interesting mementoes of Isandhlwana and Rorke's Drift.

2. Brecon Cathedral

Llanhamlach

Here is little else besides a stout towered church in an overgrown churchyard, with old tombstones and yew trees in plenty; and a pleasant inn beyond which is a path leading down to an old ford across the Usk.

3. Elizabethan effigy in Brecon Cathedral

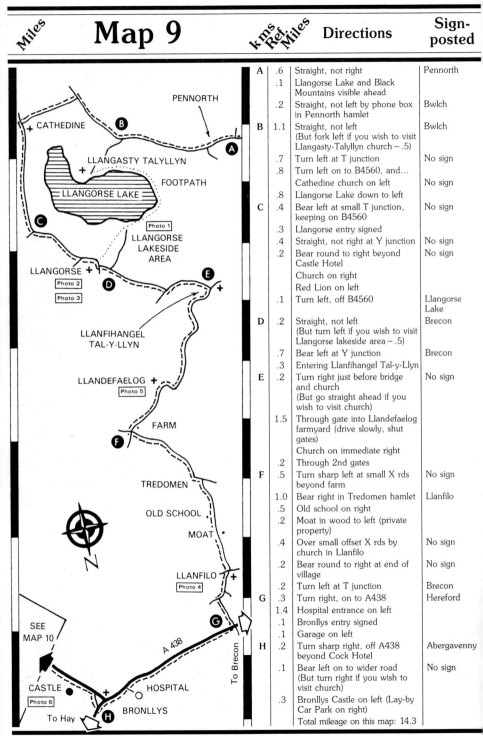

Map 9

	kms Ref Miles	Directions	Sign-posted
A	.6	Straight, not right	Pennorth
	.1	Llangorse Lake and Black Mountains visible ahead	
	.2	Straight, not left by phone box in Pennorth hamlet	Bwlch
B	1.1	Straight, not left (But fork left if you wish to visit Llangasty-Talyllyn church – .5)	Bwlch
	.7	Turn left at T junction	No sign
	.8	Turn left on to B4560, and...	
		Cathedine church on left	No sign
	.8	Llangorse Lake down to left	
C	.4	Bear left at small T junction, keeping on B4560	No sign
	.3	Llangorse entry signed	
	.4	Straight, not right at Y junction	No sign
	.2	Bear round to right beyond Castle Hotel	No sign
		Church on right	
		Red Lion on left	
	.1	Turn left, off B4560	Llangorse Lake
D	.2	Straight, not left (But turn left if you wish to visit Llangorse lakeside area – .5)	Brecon
	.7	Bear left at Y junction	Brecon
	.3	Entering Llanfihangel Tal-y-Llyn	
E	.2	Turn right just before bridge and church (But go straight ahead if you wish to visit church)	No sign
	1.5	Through gate into Llandefaelog farmyard (drive slowly, shut gates)	
		Church on immediate right	
	.2	Through 2nd gates	
F	.5	Turn sharp left at small X rds beyond farm	No sign
	1.0	Bear right in Tredomen hamlet	Llanfilo
	.5	Old school on right	
	.2	Moat in wood to left (private property)	
	.4	Over small offset X rds by church in Llanfilo	No sign
	.2	Bear round to right at end of village	No sign
	.2	Turn left at T junction	Brecon
G	.3	Turn right, on to A438	Brecon Hereford
	1.4	Hospital entrance on left	
	.1	Bronllys entry signed	
	.1	Garage on left	
H	.2	Turn sharp right, off A438 beyond Cock Hotel	Abergavenny
	.1	Bear left on to wider road (But turn right if you wish to visit church)	No sign
	.3	Bronllys Castle on left (Lay-by Car Park on right)	
		Total mileage on this map: 14.3	

18

To Llangorse Lake, below the Black Mountains

Llangorse Lake

This is the largest natural lake in South Wales and was formed by glacial action. For those who value tranquillity the best access is by the path from Llangasty Talyllyn (see below). However if you wish to go boating or fishing, the lively lakeside area beyond Llangorse Common (turn left at Point D) will be your objective. Here will be found ample parking space and a variety of facilities including camping and caravan sites, boat hire, shop, etc.

1. Spring sunshine at Llangorse Lake

Llangasty Talyllyn

This is a Victorian hamlet on the southern shore of Llangorse Lake. The church is a real period piece, having been designed by J. L. Pearson, the architect of Truro Cathedral; and although pitch-pine pews and shiny tiles predominate, the elaborately decorated chancel deserves a visit. There is a footpath from here around the reed bordered western shore of Llangorse Lake to Llangorse Common, and this provides fine opportunities to spot a wide variety of birds including Canada geese in winter, and reed warblers and great crested grebes in summer.

Cathedine

Small hamlet beneath Mynydd Llangorse, with lovely views of the lake from its sloping churchyard. The little church appears to be entirely Victorian.

Llangorse Village

Pleasant village with a small hotel, and an inn below the church, past which a small stream flows.

2. Llangorse Church

3. Stream in Llangorse village

Llanfihangel Tal-y-Llyn

An unexceptional village with its church tucked away behind the Black Cock Inn. The pleasant red sandstone exterior encloses a disappointing interior, dark with stained glass, but relieved by an interesting little font with ropework.

Llandefaelog

Here is a gated, grassy farmyard, with a pleasant little, long low church overshadowed by massive yews. The unspoilt interior contains two attractive 18th century monuments and an old chest.

Llanfilo

Attractive little village with a single sloping street, at the head of which stands a small shingle-spired church beyond a pleasant lych gate. The white washed interior contains many items of interest including a splendid rood screen, which like the rest of the church, has been most sympathetically restored.

4. Rood screen detail, Llanfilo

Bronllys

A small village astride the ever busy A438, with a church which has a detached tower, reminding us that we are not far away from the borders of Herefordshire, where there are no fewer than seven out of England's total of forty detached towers. The interior contains an interesting old font and a fine Jacobean pulpit brought here from Llandefaelog. Bronllys Castle lies just beyond the village and consists only of a stout 13th century round tower. However there are fine views out across the valley to the Black Mountains rising above Talgarth.

5. Llandefaelog Church

6. Bronllys Castle

Miles	Ref	Directions	Signposted
.2		Talgarth entry signed	
.2		Over offset X-rds	Abergavenny
.3		Bear left, in Talgarth Centre and...	No sign
	A	Straight, not right by Church Hall	No sign
		(But turn right to visit church – .1, and/or Llanelieu church – 2.5. See separate route directions opposite)	
		Leave Talgarth on main road	
.3		Turn right onto A4078	Three Cocks
1.4	B	Turn right, off A4078	Felindre
1.0		Straight, not left	No sign
.5		Old Gwernyfed Manor on left	
.1		Straight, not right by the Three Horseshoes in Felindre	No sign
		Bear left, and then...	
.1	C	Fork right by village hall	No sign
.4		Fork left, keeping on wider road	Tregoyd
.2		Straight, not right at Y junction	Tregoyd
.4		Straight, not left, beyond Tregoyd Activity Centre	Hay
.5	D	Over small X rds	Hay
.3		Fforddlas entry signed	
.1		Straight, not right at Y junction by phone box, and...	No sign
		Straight, not right, again	Hay
.2		Bear round to right at T junction	No sign
.7	E	Straight, not right	Hay
		(But turn right if you wish to visit Llanigon church – .1)	
.3		Bear right at T junction near end of village	Hay
1.0		Turn right at T junction, on to B4350	Hay
.2		Hay-on-Wye entry signed	
.4	F	Bear left keeping on B4350 (WE ARE JOINED HERE FROM THE END OF MAP 15)	Hereford
.1		Straight, not left by Swan Hotel (But turn sharp left if you wish to visit church and Bailey Walk – .1)	No sign
.1		Turn right, on to B4348. (We shall keep on B4348 for 5 miles)	Bredwardine
		Castle on left (private). Car Park on right. (Park here and explore town on foot)	
.1		Straight, not left	No sign
.2		Bear round to right keeping on B4348	Bredwardine
		Over bridge, and...	
.1	G	Straight, not right	No sign
.2		Straight, not left, at exit from Hay	No sign
.2		Straight, not right at T junction on bend	Bredwardine
		Total mileage on this map: 9.2	

Into Kilvert Country and a town of books

Talgarth

Busy little market town beneath the western slopes of the Black Mountains, with its market place overlooked by a small Victorian Town Hall and an interesting medieval tower, rather similar to the Pele towers of the north country. The church has a tall well proportioned medieval tower, but the interior has been over restored. The large incised tomb slab in the south aisle chapel is said to be that of the local saint, St. Gwendoline.

1. Llanelieu Church

Llanelieu

This simple little building is in a lovely setting below the hills and has a delightfully unspoilt interior, including a primitive rood screen with tympanum stretching right up to the roof.

(To reach Llanelieu turn right, off main route by Talgarth Church Hall, right by church tower, left by churchyard gate, up Church Street, fork right [signed Llanelieu], straight, not right, walk up right beyond farm with gothic doorway [ask here for church key]. The road is narrow and should only be used if you wish to visit the church. Drive slowly.)

2. Old Gwernyfed

Old Gwernyfed

Splendid 17th century manor house (now a hotel), with a 13th century doorway. The house was built in about 1610 by Sir David Williams, a court physician, and Charles I stayed here shortly after the battle of Naseby.

Llanigon

Minute village with a small creeper covered church. This has a massive 14th century south porch, with great bells hanging in its barn-like roof. It was to Llanigon that Francis Kilvert came in vain to court his Daisy Thomas (read *Kilvert's Diary* for its wonderfully evocative descriptions of the local 19th century scene… see also Bredwardine, page 23).

Hay-on-Wye

Charming market town situated between the north-western slopes of the Black Mountains and the high banks of the lovely river Wye… here crossed by a tall, but rather dull concrete bridge (Offa's Dyke Long-distance Path crosses the Wye here… see page 29). There is a wealth of unpretentious 18th and early 19th century houses, shops and inns, all at different levels. The church, apart from its tower, was rebuilt in 1833, but although it has a stylish interior, it is not of great interest. Between the church and the mound of Hay's original castle, there is a path leading down to the attractive Bailey Walk, beside the Wye. The later castle was incorporated into a 17th century mansion, and this overlooks the lively little market place.

Following the pattern set several years ago by secondhand bookseller extraordinary, Richard Booth, there are now a multitude of book shops in Hay. Anyone with more than a passing interest in books should stop here and be prepared to forsake the roads a while. Browsers could come away from Hay considerably richer in mind, if not in pocket!

3. The Church porch, Llanigon

4. Bargain-hunting at Hay

5. The Wye from Bailey Walk, Hay

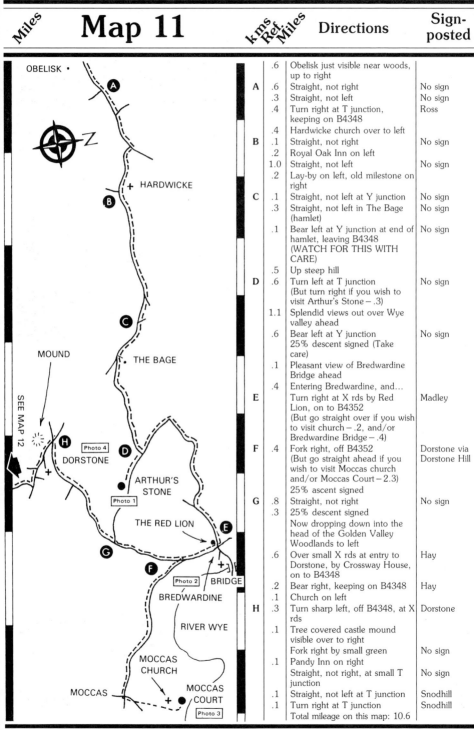

		.6	Obelisk just visible near woods, up to right	
	A	.6	Straight, not right	No sign
		.3	Straight, not left	No sign
		.4	Turn right at T junction, keeping on B4348	Ross
		.4	Hardwicke church over to left	
	B	.1	Straight, not right	No sign
		.2	Royal Oak Inn on left	
		1.0	Straight, not left	No sign
		.2	Lay-by on left, old milestone on right	
	C	.1	Straight, not left at Y junction	No sign
		.3	Straight, not left in The Bage (hamlet)	No sign
		.1	Bear left at Y junction at end of hamlet, leaving B4348 (WATCH FOR THIS WITH CARE)	No sign
		.5	Up steep hill	
	D	.6	Turn left at T junction (But turn right if you wish to visit Arthur's Stone – .3)	No sign
		1.1	Splendid views out over Wye valley ahead	
		.6	Bear left at Y junction 25% descent signed (Take care)	No sign
		.1	Pleasant view of Bredwardine Bridge ahead	
		.4	Entering Bredwardine, and…	
	E		Turn right at X rds by Red Lion, on to B4352 (But go straight over if you wish to visit church – .2, and/or Bredwardine Bridge – .4)	Madley
	F	.4	Fork right, off B4352 (But go straight ahead if you wish to visit Moccas church and/or Moccas Court – 2.3) 25% ascent signed	Dorstone via Dorstone Hill
	G	.8	Straight, not right	No sign
		.3	25% descent signed	
			Now dropping down into the head of the Golden Valley Woodlands to left	
		.6	Over small X rds at entry to Dorstone, by Crossway House, on to B4348	Hay
		.2	Bear right, keeping on B4348	Hay
		.1	Church on left	
	H	.3	Turn sharp left, off B4348, at X rds	Dorstone
		.1	Tree covered castle mound visible over to right	
			Fork right by small green	No sign
		.1	Pandy Inn on right	
			Straight, not right, at small T junction	No sign
		.1	Straight, not left at T junction	Snodhill
		.1	Turn right at T junction	Snodhill
			Total mileage on this map: 10.6	

Through Kilvert's Bredwardine to the Golden Valley

Hardwicke

Hamlet with a modest inn and a small 19th century church, which does not appear to be of great interest to visitors.

Arthur's Stone

These great stones (the description 'Arthur's Stone', is to say the least, inaccurate) are the remains of a prehistoric long barrow... a burial chamber which was once covered by a long mound of earth.

1. Arthur's Stone

Bredwardine

A small village, but what a wealth of interest and beauty it contains... first the Red Lion Hotel, a handsome late 17th century building of mellow brick... and then, leaving the main route, the church. Before looking round, go inside and purchase the exceptionally well produced and helpful guide to both church and village. Here will be revealed the interesting features of the church (including the Norman south doorway, the massive Norman font, the carved lintel of a blocked Norman north doorway and the two effigies in the chancel)... the path to the castle mound, the old vicarage where the diarist Francis Kilvert (see also Llanigon, page 21) lived as vicar from 1877 until his death two years later at the early age of 38... Kilvert's gravestone to the north of the church tower and the path over the fields down to the six arched brick bridge over the gently curving Wye.

2. Bredwardine Bridge

Moccas

(Go straight ahead on B4352 from Point F for 1.7, turn left by war memorial, after .1, bear left into Moccas Park, go down drive slowly, turning left for church. Go beyond if Moccas Court is open.)

Here in broad parkland is a perfect little Norman church with apsidal chancel. Here are Norman doorways, two lovely arches, with the stone effigy of a knight between them, and also some attractive 14th century glass. Moccas Court (see Opening Times), beautifully sited above the Wye, is a handsome mellow brick mansion built to the designs of Robert Adam in 1775 – 1781. The interior is a treasure house of 18th century decoration and should on no account be missed.

3. Moccas Court

The Golden Valley

The easternmost and least wild of a series of valleys running south-eastwards from the high north-western edge of the Black Mountains.

Dorstone

A pleasant village near the head of the Golden Valley with the earthworks of a small motte and bailey castle to the immediate west of a small tidy green. Here will be found the attractive little Pandy Inn, a cheerful Post Office stores and a modern sundial on an old stone pillar. The rather uninteresting Victorian church stands on the foundations of an earlier building, established in the 12th century by Thomas de Brito, who retired to this remote valley as a penance for the murder, along with three other knights, of Archbishop Becket.

4. The village green, Dorstone

(Map showing SNODHILL, CASTLE RUINS, FINE STREET, OLD LIMEKILN, HINTON, PETERCHURCH, TURNASTONE, VOWCHURCH, POST OFFICE, ST. MARGARETS, INN, NEWTON, BACTON, SEE MAP 13; with markers A–H, Photo 1–5, and compass N)

Ref.	Miles	Directions	Sign-posted
A	.7	Turn left at X rds in Snodhill	Peterchurch
	.2	Snodhill castle ruins up to right	
	.1	Pleasant view of Golden Valley over to left	
	.2	Turn right at T junction	No sign
	.7	Old limekiln over to right	
	.1	Straight, not right, in Fine Street hamlet	
B	.6	Turn left at X rds in Hinton hamlet	Peterchurch
	.3	Turn right at X rds re-joining B4348 by the Nag's Head Inn, at entry to Peterchurch	No sign
	.1	Border Craft Workshops on right	
	.2	Straight, not right by the Boughton Arms Hotel (But turn right if you wish to visit church – .1)	No sign
C	.3	Over X rds	Vowchurch
	.5	Vowchurch entry signed (no sign of village yet)	
	.9	Turn right into Vowchurch at X rds, off B4348	Vowchurch
	.2	Vowchurch church on left, and…	
		Over bridge	
	.1	Turnastone entry signed	
	.2	Church on right	
	.1	Petrol Station and Post Office on left	
D	.8	Straight, not right near bend	No sign
	1.1	Open country on right	
	.3	Straight, not left at T junction	No sign
E	.2	Turn left at T junction by Methodist chapel	No sign
	.8	Straight, not left at Y junction	No sign
	.2	Turn left at T junction	No sign
	.4	Bear left at T junction	No sign
	.1	St. Margaret's Post Office on right	
F	.2	Turn right at T junction	No sign
	.6	St. Margaret's church on right (DON'T MISS THIS)	
	.2	Sun Inn on right	
		Fine views of Black Mountains ahead	
G	.5	Turn left at X rds (But go straight ahead if you wish to visit Newton church – .2)	Bacton
	.7	Turn left at X rds	Bacton
	1.1	Bear left in Bacton (But turn up right if you wish to visit church)	No sign
H	.4	Turn right on to B4347	Pontrilas
		Total mileage on this map: 13.1	

On the Black Mountains' eastern fringes

Snodhill
A quiet hamlet with a pleasing 17th century farmhouse, and just beyond it, the ivy clad ruins of a 14th century castle on a steep sided hillock overlooking the Golden Valley.

Peterchurch
A long straggling village astride the B4348, with the little River Dore running parallel just to the east. The slender spire was only rebuilt a few years ago, but inside there is impressive evidence of the church's Norman origins... a sequence of three tall Norman arches ending in an apsidal chancel. See also the Norman north doorway, the Norman tub font and the plump plaster mould of a cheerful looking carp... it could only happen in Herefordshire!

Vowchurch
Minute village with a small church overlooking the River Dore, and just beyond, a 16th century half timbered 'old vicarage'. Inside the church will be found a roof supported on fascinating timber posts. Both these and the rood screen were by John Abel (1613), better known for his work at Abbey Dore (see page 27).

Turnastone
Even smaller than its neighbour Vowchurch, Turnastone has a friendly little Post Office stores and an attractive, long low church, with an elegant little Jacobean pulpit, a pretty 17th century wall monument and an incised tomb slab of a 16th century knight and his lady.

St. Margaret's
A beautifully quiet hamlet in the hills with wide views westwards to the flanks of the mountains rising above the upper Monnow valley. Beside the churchyard there is a small farm, and there is a cheerful inn just beyond. Inside the church, with its little weatherboarded belfry oversailing the west end, will be found one of the finest rood screens and lofts in the whole Border Country, with beautifully carved woodwork, all about 1520. See also the carefully renovated wall paintings, the Jacobean altar rail and the pleasant old font cover.

Newton
The small church here was built in 1842, and apart from the Jacobean pulpit, the contents are all contemporary with the building... a period piece for lovers of this particular style only.

Bacton
The church in this hamlet has a large stout tower and an early Perpendicular door within its south porch. The heavily restored interior contains three items of interest... a beautifully embroidered 17th century altar frontal, a small 17th century wall monument with two kneeling figures, and most impressive of all, a monument to Blanche Parry, Maid of Honour to Queen Elizabeth 1st, with both Blanche and her Queen portrayed in effigy.

1. Snodhill Castle   2. Queen Bess at Bacton

3. Vowchurch Church

4. The Black Mountains from St. Margaret's churchyard

5. Rood screen detail, St. Margaret's

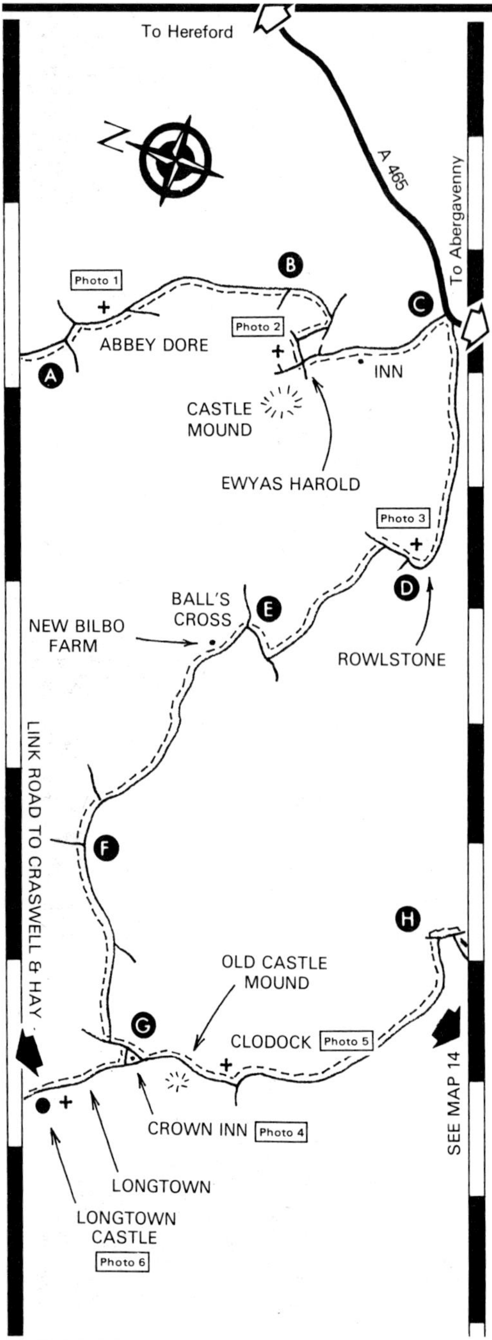

To Hereford

A 465

To Abergavenny

Photo 1

B

C

Photo 2

ABBEY DORE

INN

A

CASTLE MOUND

EWYAS HAROLD

Photo 3

BALL'S CROSS

E

D

NEW BILBO FARM

ROWLSTONE

LINK ROAD TO CRASWELL & HAY

F

H

OLD CASTLE MOUND

G

CLODOCK   Photo 5

CROWN INN   Photo 4

SEE MAP 14

LONGTOWN

LONGTOWN CASTLE

Photo 6

Ref	Miles	Directions	Signposted
	.8	Abbey Dore church visible ahead	
	.3	Abbey Dore entry signed	
A	.1	Turn left, and…	Pontrilas
		Bear right, keeping on B4347 (But turn left if you wish to visit Abbey Dore Court Gardens… .3)	Pontrilas
	.3	Abbey church down to left	
	.1	Neville Arms up to right	
	.1	Straight, not right at Y junction	No sign
B	.7	Straight, not right	No sign
	.1	Ewyas Harold entry signed	
	.3	Straight, not left at Y junction	Pontrilas
	.1	Fork right, off B4347. (WATCH FOR THIS WITH CARE)	No sign
	.2	Turn left at T junction	No sign
	.1	Bear left by phone box (But turn right and right again if you wish to visit church)	Pontrilas
	.1	Bear right, re-joining B4347	Pontrilas
C	.8	Turn right on to A465, and almost immediately…	Abergavenny
	.1	Fork right, off A465 just BEFORE garage	Rowlstone
	1.3	Bear right at T junction	No sign
	.2	Enter Rowlstone	
	.1	Church up to right	
D	.1	Straight, not left just beyond church	Ball's Cross
	.2	Bear left at Y junction	No sign
	.9	Turn right at T junction	Ball's Cross
E	.3	Turn left at T junction (This is Ball's Cross, but nothing to identify it)	Longtown
	.1	New Bilbo Farm to right	
	1.2	Straight, not right, at Y junction, on to wider road	Longtown
F	.3	Straight, not right	Longtown
	.5	Bear right at T junction, and… Start to descend steep hill	No sign
	.1	Fine views out over the Monnow valley	
	.4	Over the Escley Brook, and…	
	.1	Turn left at T junction, and… Over the Monnow	Longtown
G	.2	Bear left, keeping on wider road, by the Crown Inn, Longtown, and	No sign

(BUT TURN RIGHT AND RIGHT AGAIN, IF YOU WISH TO VISIT LONGTOWN. CASTLE – .6. OR IF YOU WISH TO EXPLORE THE MONNOW VALLEY, UP TO CRASWALL, AND OVER TO HAY, LINKING WITH MAP 15, POINT G, 9 MILES)

Ref	Miles	Directions	Signposted
		Bear left again beyond inn	Clodock
	.2	Over Pont Hendre. Castle mound to right	
	.4	Clodock church on left, and… Straight, not right, just beyond Cornewall Arms on left	Walterstone
	.1	Over bridge crossing the Monnow	
H	1.6	Bear round to right at small T junction	No sign
	.1	Bear right at T junction	Pandy
		Total mileage on this map: 12.6	

26

Fascinating churches and a stout border castle

1. Abbey Dore

Abbey Dore

Here, in this small village in the Golden valley, is preserved the entire eastern end of a great church, part of a Cistercian abbey founded here in 1147. After the Dissolution in 1539, the abbey and its church soon fell into decay, but Lord Scudamore and his architect craftsman, John Abel, restored all but the great nave of the church. Here then is an example of an Early English abbey church, with beautiful 17th century furnishings and glass... a wonderfully satisfying and outstandingly interesting building, which should on no account be missed.

Ewyas Harold

Colourful little village with two lively inns. The Dulas brook flows beside the church, which has a stout 13th century tower and over restored interior, and which is overlooked by the fragmentary ruins of William Fitzosbern's great castle on a high wooded mound to the north-west.

Rowlstone

The pitch-pine pews and tidy minds of the Victorian restorers have not destroyed the atmosphere of the fascinating little Norman church. There is a Norman south doorway, with birds on the capitals, topped by a splendid Norman tympanum depicting the Christ in Majesty. The chancel arch is also richly carved, with birds on the capitals, and on the south side, an angel and a bishop upside down... a stone mason's error, or was there some hidden meaning? See also the unique late medieval candle bracket.

2. Ewyas Harold Church

3. 'Christ-in-Majesty' tympanum, Rowlstone

Longtown

Attractive village in the broad Monnow valley. The white painted Crown Inn (built 1751) looks particularly pleasant. The largely Victorian church appears to be derelict, but the castle with its fine circular keep and rectangular outer bailey earthworks are in the care of English Heritage and are open at any reasonable time. This castle almost certainly superseded an earlier one, built soon after the conquest at the southern end of the village (see Route Directions).

The Upper Monnow Valley to Craswall... diversion (See Map 15)

This road up the Monnow valley from Longtown provides a less busy alternative to our route up the Honddu valley on Map 15. The ruins of 13th century Craswall Priory are about a mile off the road, well beyond Craswall church. They are in a bad state of repair and should be left undisturbed.

Clodock

Here is a cheerful little inn and a largely Norman church in a churchyard running down to the banks of the little River Monnow. The church has a fascinating interior with much 17th and 18th century woodwork, including a west gallery, pews, stalls and a fine three decker pulpit behind which is an incised tomb slab, probably as early as the ninth century in origin. See also the wide Norman chancel arch and the beautifully lettered slate tablets beneath the gallery.

4. The Crown Inn, Longtown

5. From Clodock Porch

6. Longtown Castle

Map labels:

INN
Photo 1
WALTERSTONE
CASTLE MOUND
ALLT-YR-YNYS
RIVER MONNOW
TREWYN
To Llanthony on Map 15
OFFA'S DYKE LONG-DISTANCE PATH
CWMYOY
To Grwyne Fawr Valley — Photo 2
QUEEN'S HEAD INN
BRYNARW
To Partishow Church — Photo 4 — Photo 5
CAR PARK
FOREST COAL PIT
BLAENAWEY
PATH
THE SUGAR LOAF
To Abergavenny

Ref	Miles	Directions	Signposted
	.6	Enter Walterstone hamlet Carpenter's Arms and church on left, and...	
		Straight, not left, and...	No sign
		Small castle mound on right	
	.5	Fine view of Skirrid ahead left	
	.7	Straight, not left, at entry to Allt-yr-Ynys hamlet	Pandy
	.1	Over bridge crossing Monnow, re-entering Wales	
A	.3	Over offset X rds crossing wider road	Trewyn
	.2	Through Trewyn hamlet	
	.1	Up steep narrow road with great care	
	.3	Offa's Dyke Long-distance Path comes down from right and follows our road for .3	
	.3	Over small X rds. Offa's Dyke path goes to left	No sign
	.3	Now dropping down into Honddu valley	
	.3	Turn sharp left at T junction	No sign
	.1	Over bridge crossing Honddu	
B	.1	Bear left by Queen's Head Inn	No sign

(BUT TURN *VERY SHARP RIGHT* IF YOU WISH TO START MAP 15. N.B. IF THIS IS TOO SHARP FOR YOU, TURN LEFT AND THEN FIND A PLACE TO TURN ABOUT BEFORE STARTING MAP 15. *PLEASE READ NOTE AT HEAD OF PAGE 30 BEFORE MAKING A DECISION*)

Ref	Miles	Directions	Signposted
C	.3	Turn right at T junction in Brynarw	Forest Coal P
	1.1	Into pleasant wooded country	
D	.7	Turn first left at 5 way cross (But go straight ahead, turn right, and bear right if you wish to visit Partrishow Church — 1.3. N.B. narrow road, parking space very limited) (But turn right if you wish to drive up Grwyne Fawr valley to Mynydd Ddu Forest Car Park, etc 3.1)	Forest Coal P
	.2	Enter Forest Coal Pit Hamlet	
E	.1	Bear left at Y junction just beyond cottage	Abergavenny
	.1	Bear right at Y junction	No sign
	.1	Straight, not left just before Post Office	No sign
	.5	Car Park on right, for path to the Sugar Loaf — 2.5 miles)	
	.6	Through Blaenawey hamlet	
F	.9	Bear right on to wider road	Abergavenny
	.1	Crown Inn on right	
		NOW OFF MAP	
	.9	Straight, not left	Abergavenny
	.5	Entering Abergavenny	
	.7	Bear left keeping on wider road	No sign
	.2	Turn left, on to ring road	No sign
	.1	Straight, not right, keeping on ring road	No sign
	.1	Turn right at T junction	Monmouth
	.2	Church on left	
G	.1	Turn left at traffic lights by the Angel Hotel	Monmouth

LINKING WITH MAP 1, POINT A
Total mileage on this map: 11.4

Below the Black Mountains to the Sugar Loaf

Walterstone

This hamlet is blessed with a marvellous little inn... a freehouse called the Carpenter's Arms, which has a parlour complete with black-leaded 'kitchen' fireplace and a real flavour of times gone by. Call here for a drink, but first borrow the key to the small church, which lies just beyond. Its interior has been heavily restored, but its simplicity has not been spoilt, and here are charming views southwards to the Skirrid mountain from the churchyard.

Allt-yr-Ynys

Pleasant tree shaded hamlet marking our return to Wales, as we cross the sparkling River Monnow. The lovely stone Tudor house of Allt-yr-Ynys* was once the family home of the Sitsyllts, later to become known as the Cecils, the first of whom to gain high office being Robert Cecil, created Lord Burleigh by Queen Elizabeth 1st

On our left just before the bridge

Offa's Dyke Long-distance Path

Prestatyn to Chepstow... 168 miles)

Although there are no visible remains of Offa's Dyke in the area covered by this guide, Offa's Dyke Long-distance Path follows our road for a short distance (beyond Trewyn), and the 'Ridge Route' N.N.W. from here up to Hay Bluff and down to Hay makes a fine walk. (Do not attempt without reading advice on page 13.) Offa's Dyke was probably constructed between AD 750–800 as a boundary between the Saxon Kingdom of Mercia and the Welsh hills, and the best sections, with classic bank and ditch, are to be found in the area of Presteigne and Knighton well to the north.

Partrishow

A simple little building hidden away on a remote hillside far above the Grwyne Fawr valley, with the sounds of rushing water, and the bleat of sheep never far away. Inside will be found one of the finest medieval rood screens in Wales, and also two incised medieval altar slabs in the floor, a wall painting of Old Father Time, a pleasant Jacobean pulpit and a massive early Norman font. Parking is a great problem and the walk up the church is very steep, but the effort is well worthwhile.

The Grwyne Fawr Valley

It is three miles up this narrow and attractively wooded valley to the first Forestry Commission car park and picnic site, from which there is a pleasant forest walk; and a further three miles to another picnic site at the head of the public road. There is a fine path from here above the Grwyne Fawr Reservoir and over the mountains to Talgarth (Map 10).

The Sugar Loaf

Splendid 1,955 feet high, conical shaped mountain, that dominates Abergavenny and much of the middle Usk valley. There are several routes up it, the best known leading from a 1,000 foot high car park signed off the Abergavenny–Brecon road. However a quieter approach is from the car park beyond Forest Coal Pit on our route, and this is recommended.

1. The Carpenter's Arms, Walterstone

2. Picnic Site, Mynydd Ddu Forest

3. Churchyard in the hills, Partrishow

4. Pathway to Partrishow Church

5. Old Father Time at Partrishow

Map 15

MAIN ROUTE MAP 14

A QUEEN'S HEAD, BRYNARW

WALTERSTONE

Photo 1

CWMYOY

B DIALGARREG

FAWR

GRWYNE DIVERSION

MAIN ROUTE, MAP 13

C

LLANTHONY

Photo 2

Photo 3

LONGTOWN

PRIORY

HALF MOON HOTEL

GATEHOUSE

(NOTE DIFFERENT SCALE ON THIS MAP)

MONASTERY

D Photo 5

Photo 4

CAPEL-Y-FFIN

GOSPEL PASS

CRASWALL

Photo 6

CRASWALL PRIORY

HAY BLUFF

E LORD HEREFORD'S KNOB

F

G

MAIN ROUTE, MAP 10

HAY **H**

	kms. Ref. Miles	Directions	Sign-posted
A		Head up the Honddu Valley on the B4423, from the Queen's Head, Brynarw (2 miles N.W. of Llanfihangel Crucorney) (This is common with Map 14, Point B)	No sign

N.B. TRY TO AVOID THIS ROUTE ON A SUNDAY, OR AT ANY BUSY HOLIDAY PERIOD. IT SHOULD PREFERABLY BE EXPLORED ON AN AUTUMN, WINTER OR SPRING WEEKDAY, AND THEN ONLY WITH CARE AND CONSIDERATION FOR OTHER ROAD USERS.

	kms. Ref. Miles	Directions	Sign-posted
	.8	Path to Cwmyoy on right (park here and walk in preference to using road from Point B, as there is only limited parking space in Cwmyoy)	
B	.5	Straight, not right	No sign
	.6	Path up left to Dialgarreg	
	.2	Rocky crags visible up to right	
	.8	Lay-by on left	
	.2	Path up left to Bal-Bach Baptist Chapel on right	
	.6	Llanthony Wood to left	
	.5	Over River Honddu	
C	.4	Straight, not right in Llanthony hamlet. (But turn right if you wish to visit Llanthony Priory, church, and/or Abbey Hotel – .1)	Capel-y-Ffin
	.1	Barn on right (once the Priory Gatehouse) Half Moon Hotel on left	
	.1	Bear left at Y junction, and over Honddu	Capel-y-Ffin
	.8	Path left to Bal-Bach	
	.1	Path right to Loxidge Tump	
	.2	Lay-by on right	
	.1	Straight, not right at small T junction	No sign
	.5	Lay-by on right	
	.8	Path to Hatterall Ridge on right	
D	.6	Straight, not left, at Capel-y-Ffin (But fork left and turn left after .2, to visit 'The Monastery')	No sign
	1.0	Youth Hostel up to left	
	.5	Parking area on right	
	.3	Over cattlegrid on to open mountain country	
	.9	Over head of Gospel Pass	
	.2	Splendid views over to left	
E	1.1	Straight, not left at Y junction	No sign
F	.4	Straight, not left at Y junction	No sign
	.6	Tack Wood on left. Now starting to drop down steeply	
	.6	Over cattlegrid leaving mountain country	
G	.2	Bear left at T junction (But turn right if you wish to visit Craswall – 3 miles, or link to Longtown, on Map 13, Point G – 9 miles)	Hay-on-Wye
	1.6	Hay now visible ahead	
	.2	Straight, not left at Y junction	Hay-on-Wye
	.2	Entering Hay	
H	.2	Turn right at T junction, on to the B4350, LINKING WITH MAP 10, POINT F	Hereford
		Total mileage on this map: 15.9	

Llanthony and the lovely Honddu Valley

The Honddu Valley Route...
AN IMPORTANT NOTE

The long road up this lovely valley (as described in the route directions opposite) is very narrow in places and can easily become congested during summer weekends. If possible try to come here at non-peak times. Please accept our advice — it will help both you and the other users of this road.

Cwmyoy

This is a delicious little place... simply a church, a vicarage with a lovely terraced garden, a farm and a few cottages... all poised on a steep hillside overlooking the Honddu valley. After the last ice-age these slopes were the scene of great land slippages and Cwmyoy church was built on a mound which has proved over the centuries to be still unstable... hence the delightfully crazy angles of the tower and its massive flying buttresses. Inside there are old oil lamps, a 13th century crucifixion, and a charming epitaph to be found in the chancel, to one, Thomas Price... 'he takes his nap'... etc!

Dialgarreg (The Revenge Stone)

Small stone said to commemorate the ambush by Welsh tribesmen, of the Norman marcher lord, Richard de Clare. This is reached by a steep path up from our road, and lies on a ridge path between the Honddu and Grwyn Fawr valleys.

Llanthony

Minute village in the Honddu valley with the wonderfully sited ruins of a 13th century Augustinian priory. Although the west claustral range incorporates a small hotel, the rest of the ruins are in the hands of the Cadw and are tidily maintained. The parish church in the original infirmary, has a simple plastered interior relieved by a pleasing series of wall monuments.

Capel-y-Ffin (The Boundary Chapel)

Here, near the head of the Honddu valley, is a small early 19th century chapel, white painted, with a little balcony running along the north side, with old benches, and short bell ropes dropping through the ceiling. In the little graveyard is a headstone carved by one of our favourite 20th century sculptors, Eric Gill... reminding us to visit the partially ruined 'monastery' on the hillside above. This was built in the 1870s by a certain J. L. Lyne, who as 'Father Ignatius', attempted to revive an Anglican form of Benedictine monasticism here. Father Ignatius died in 1908, and in 1924 the monastery was purchased by Eric Gill. For some years he and several associates worked here, at a variety of crafts, and the low attic chapel that they used for worship, may still be visited.

The Gospel Pass

Now we finally take our leave of the Honddu valley, and pass over the watershed, to start our descent through splendid open mountain country below Lord Hereford's Knob and Hay Bluff, on our way down to Hay.

1. The leaning tower, Cwmyoy

2. Hotel in Llanthony Priory ruins

3. Llanthony Priory

4. Capel-y-Ffin

5. Monastery ruins, Capel-y-Ffin

6. Our road beyond the Gospel Pass

INDEX